Overheard
at the
Museum

Let's go to the
giftshop first.

Overheard
at the
Museum

Judith Henry

UNIVERSE

For Nina and Carla

First published in the United States of America in 2000
by UNIVERSE PUBLISHING
A Division of Rizzoli International Publications, Inc.
300 Park Avenue South
New York, NY 10010

The text in this book does not necessarily express the sentiments of the
pictured subjects.

2000 2001 2002 2003 2004 2005 / 10 9 8 7 6 5 4 3 2 1

Design and photography by Judith Henry

Printed in Singapore

Introduction

During my childhood in Ohio I often visited the Cleveland Museum of Art. I'd roam the expansive galleries with my father or alone after my Saturday morning art classes. For me visiting the museum was a quiet, mostly solitary activity. I looked at the art.

Since becoming an adult and an artist, which in large part means being an observer, I find myself looking at the *people* who look at the art. People visit museums in droves these days. They're not necessarily experts or classically trained, they just enjoy the experience. Popular museum shows can sell out just like blockbuster movies. But unlike a movie theater, museum etiquette allows for audible conversation. From the sophisticated to the outrageously candid, museum visitors are vocally inspired by what they see.

Overheard at the Museum is a cultural outing. Art stimulates response, and every viewer has an opinion. Their postures and comments are celebrated in this museum tour.

J.H.

Not only does it have a wonderful collection of medieval art but it has a fabulous restaurant.

This place is huge–it requires a lifetime!

I wish someone could explain this to me.

I really love this painting but it has way too much green in it.

You can look at the show; I'll wait in the lobby.

I come back to see this often—like an old friend.

In a world
of things
this is just
another
thing.

I made
something
similar,
but
all in
shades
of red.

Where did you get those little prints you have in your bathroom?

Being crazy . . . that's the privilege of being an artist.

There are
good ones
and
bad ones.

Wonderfully magical and cosmic.

Marge has one like that, but that's the real one.

This one over here is so horizontal.

I like the light on
that—it feels like
you're in heaven.

I have two books on Georgia O'Keeffe– they're both big.

This forces you to think, and I don't really like to do that.

I am still looking
for the van Goghs.

I'd paint it differently.

Dennis!
Hands off!

Let's see if one of these looks like Eric; he's the only Egyptian we know.

There's not enough art in here.

I'm too afraid
to be an artist.

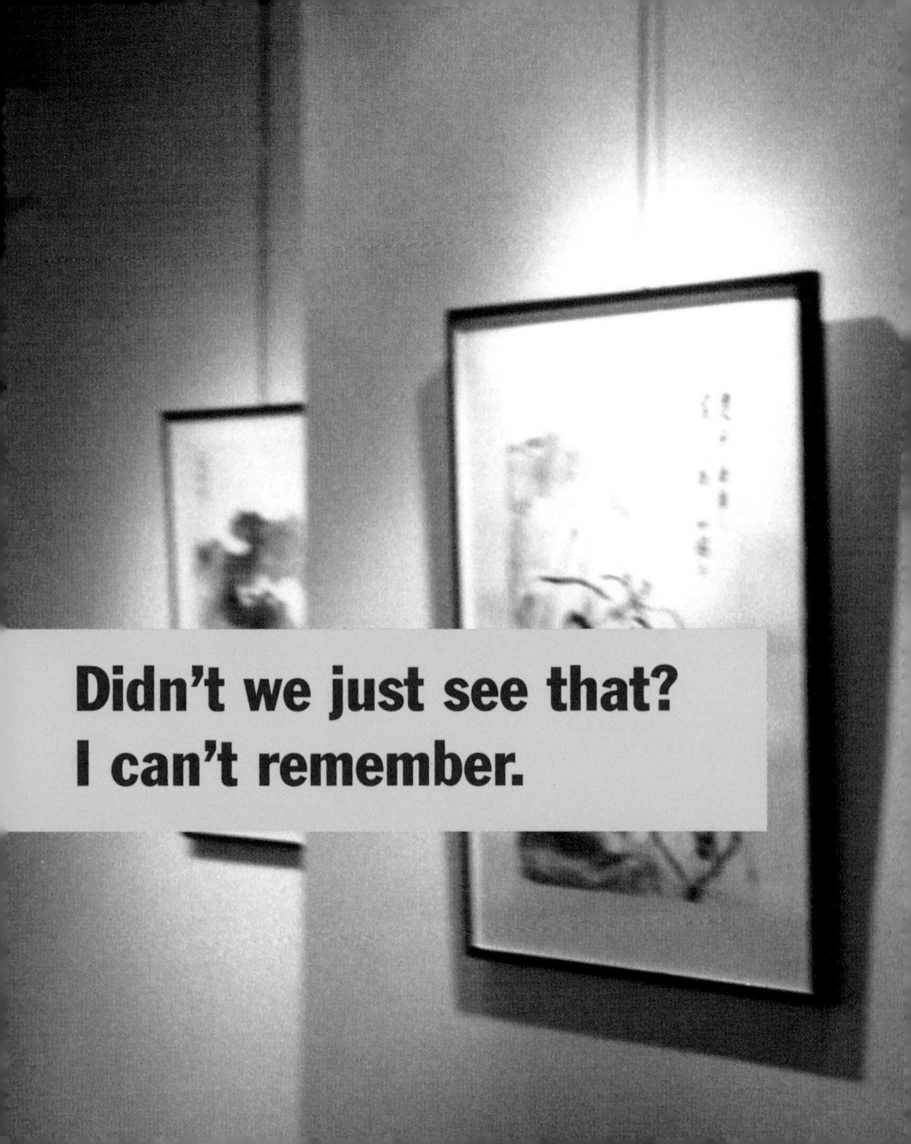
Didn't we just see that?
I can't remember.

**What
was this
before
it was
this?**

Untitled, Untitled, Untitled! Couldn't someone with so much imagination think of a title?

I wish Renoir were around to paint Jonathan.

She acts as though she has opinion and taste.

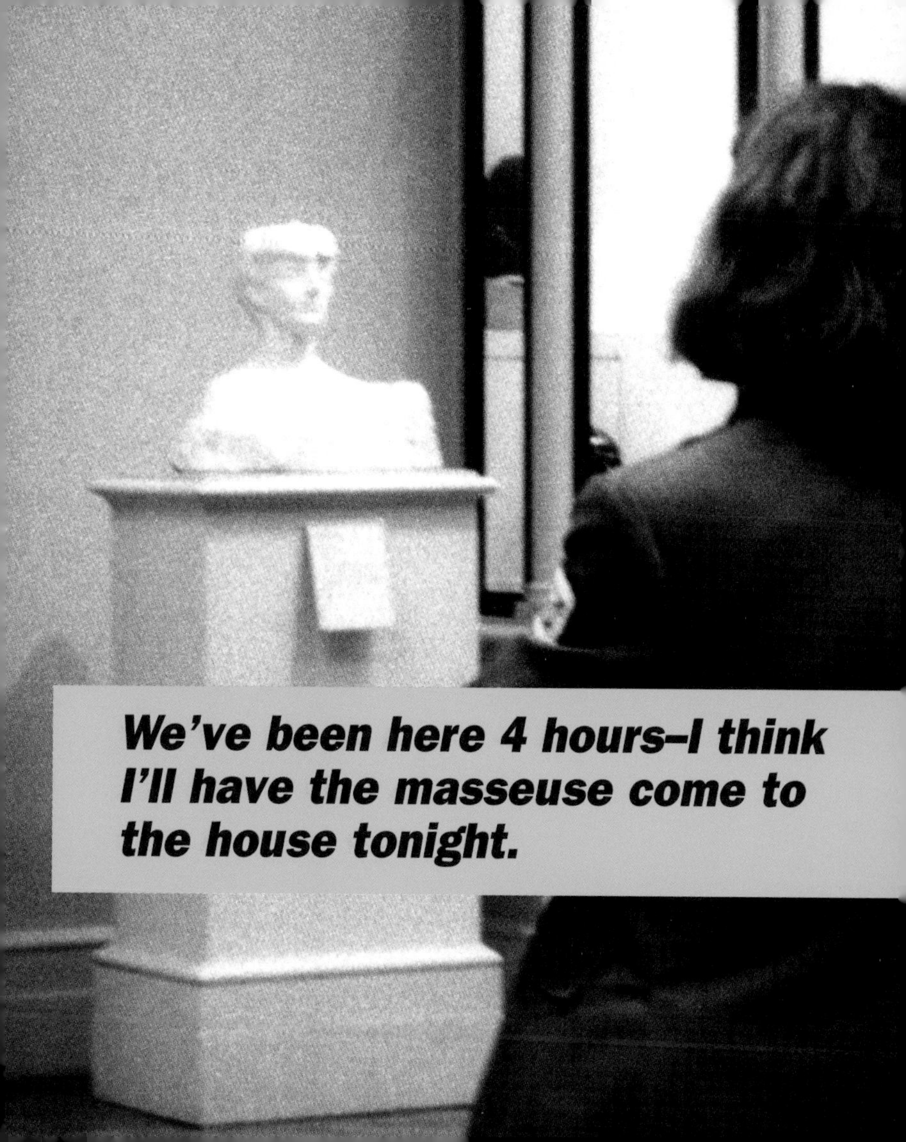
We've been here 4 hours–I think I'll have the masseuse come to the house tonight.

This work is irrelevant.

It took thousands of years to do this, and you are whipping through here in 4 seconds.

Wow! This painting is like a glass of modernist champagne.

It never received
the recognition it
deserves.

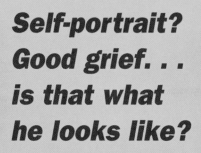

Self-portrait?
Good grief. . .
is that what
he looks like?

There's a basic level of technical inadequacy here.

And the mediocre ones sell for hundreds of thousands of dollars.

I think the postcard is better than the painting.

He never finished
it 'cause it's good
as it is now.

Dave! You're missing the most important one.

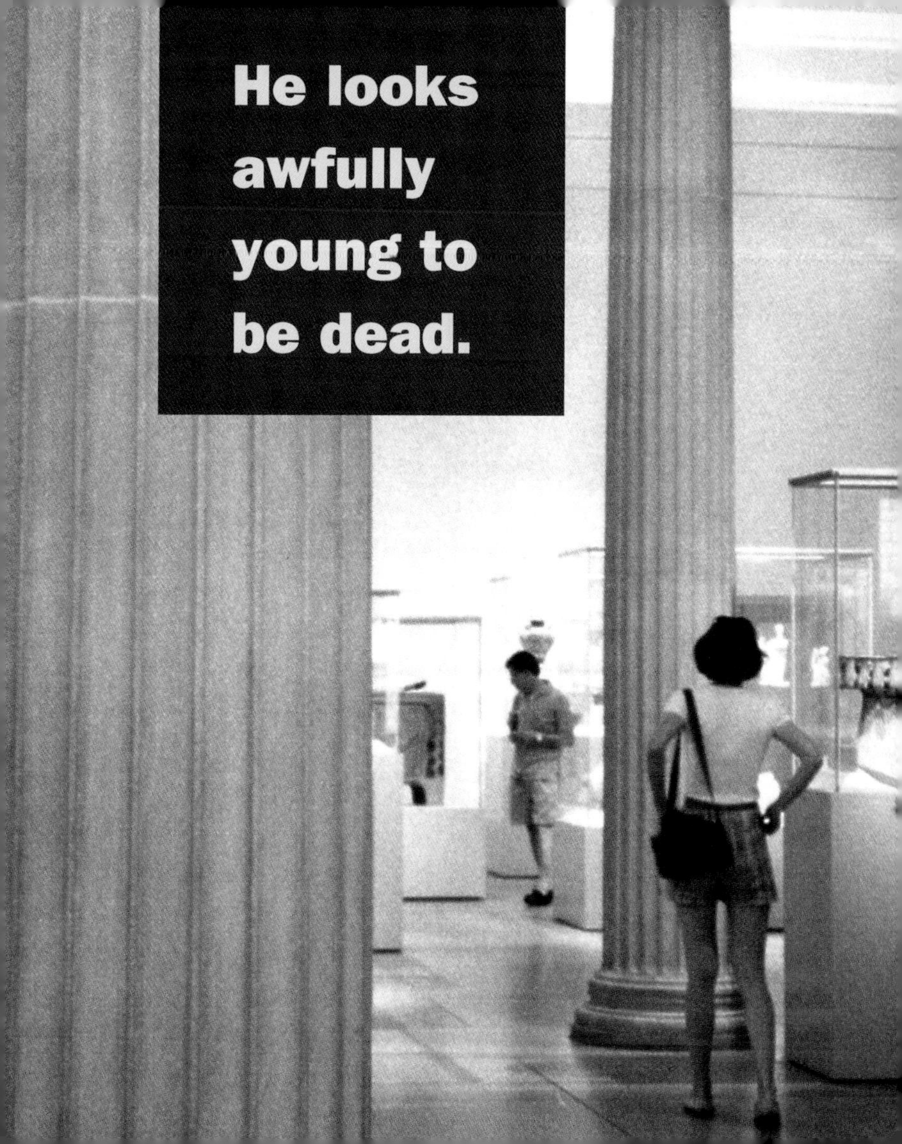
He looks awfully young to be dead.

We have five pictures
like that on our fridge.

What's it suppose to be?

Wow! Look who donated this one.

What? You don't know who Jasper Johns is?

Well, every museum makes a mistake.

I'm not going to leave until I see the Rodins.

Charlie and I are both in favor of leaving you here.

**Makes me appreciate my
little Hummel figurines.**

It feels good to sit down.

By the time you finish looking at these you need a drink.

Do you want to take a quick look at these?

Hey, You want to see the Blue period?

Can you make any sense of this one?

That's a part of the human figure I could do without deconstructing.

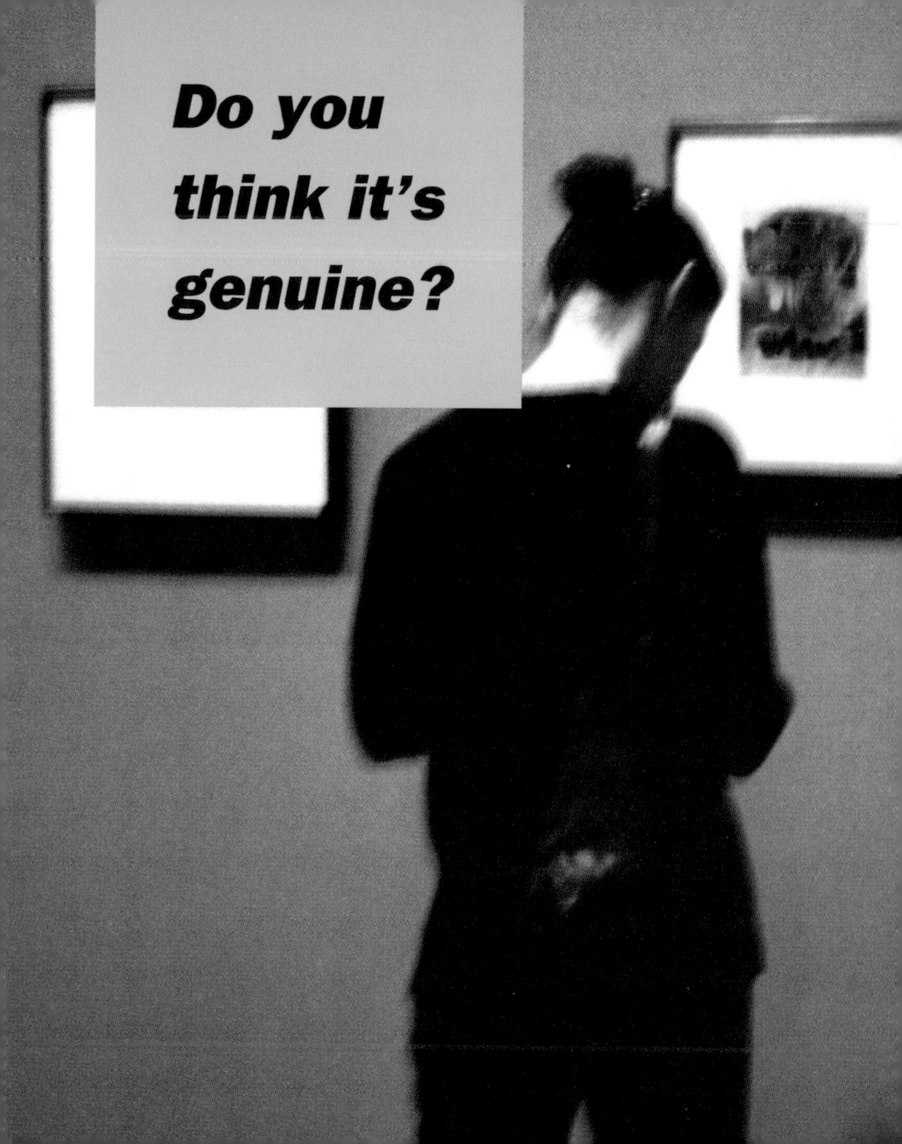
Do you think it's genuine?

How does he make little pink lines on green look like grass?

I don't care for the haystacks and I've seen them all.

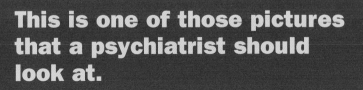

This is one of those pictures that a psychiatrist should look at.

Mediocre at best!

He made only one
statement but it was
a great one.

You think this is
easy to do?

That's just more of the same,
but you can check it out.

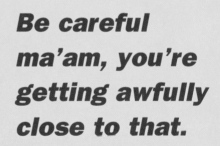

We have one of those—we should hang it up.

You're not horrified?

Why did he do the same thing twice?

I really feel tired—must be because I'm using my brain.

We had only an hour—
I saw the lobby and
that's about all.

I've seen enough
art for today.

And tomorrow we're going to see Mozart.

About the Author

Judith Henry's art has been exhibited internationally in New York, Barcelona, Buenos Aires, and London, among other places. She also designed works for The Museum of Modern Art, New York. In 1997 her book *Anonymous True Stories* was published. She lives in New York City.